GLOUCESTERSHIRE CHURCHES

EDITED BY DAVID VEREY

David Verey

Foreword by the
Bishop of Gloucester

ALAN SUTTON
1981

Alan Sutton Publishing Limited
17a Brunswick Road
Gloucester GL1 1HG

First published 1981
Published in collaboration with the Gloucestershire
Historic Churches Preservation Trust

British Library Cataloguing in Publication Data

Verey, David
   Gloucestershire churches
   1. Church architecture — England — Gloucestershire
   — History
   I. Title
   726'.5'094241   NA5469. G5
   ISBN 0-904387-80-1

Typesetting, origination and design by
Alan Sutton Publishing Limited
Photoset Bembo 10/11.5
Printed and bound in Great Britain by
Redwood Burn Limited
Trowbridge & Esher

Message from the Poet Laureate
Sir John Betjeman

Gloucestershire churches are triumphs in stone and full of variety. The Severn Valley is the cradle of English Perpendicular architecture. One good illustration is worth twenty pages of text.

January 1981.

John Betjeman

Foreword
By the Bishop of Gloucester

Much of Gloucestershire's glory is in its churches. For a thousand years and more they have testified to the Christian faith of Gloucestershire people, and they tell, in this with variety of structure and ornament, the story of Gloucestershire communities large and small, sacred and secular. Among them, and in them, one can perceive across the centuries the Anglo-Saxon mission church, the medieval abbey and parish church, the restorations and new churches of the Victorians (both Anglican and Nonconformist). And the buildings themselves are gateways in understanding to the human communities which built and cherished them (and occasionally neglected them), the Norman conqueror, the monastery, the prosperous woollen towns, the close, hard-pressed mining-villages, the busy industrial valleys of the Industrial Revolution, the lush dairy-farming hamlets, the burgeoning towns of the nineteenth and twentieth centuries. Our churches are history-books in stone and wood, glass and metal, recounting the changing fortunes of our people and their unchanging acknowledgement of Christian truth.

Christian faith and life is not in the last resort dependent on buildings of any kind, but Church people in Gloucestershire are determined that the great majority of our churches shall continue to serve the purpose for which they were built, and remain centres of living worship. However, to secure the preservation of this priceless heritage of architecture and craftsmanship now calls for a collaborative effort by many people of goodwill throughout the community. The commitment and generosity of churchgoers nowadays is stretched financially to support adequately the work of maintaining the clergy and forwarding the missionary and educational work of the Church. But many, churchgoers and non-churchgoers alike, will surely share a determination to preserve our historic churches. Support for the Gloucestershire Historic Churches Preservation Trust is a clear and obvious way to express that desire. Local communities, specially the small villages, can nowadays find themselves facing quite enormous bills for the necessary work to preserve their church. The presence of a generous and understanding friend in such circumstances not only reduces the bill but acts as a great encouragement to further effort.

On behalf of the Churches in Gloucestershire, therefore, I am deeply grateful to the men and women who have come together under the chairmanship of Sir Antony Bonham to form this Trust. This small book, the work of David Verey (that incomparably learned friend and champion of all Gloucestershire churches) and his able colleagues, will, I hope, introduce many people to the existence and work of the Trust, and encourage them to support it. I gladly commend it.

+ John G Loucesk:

Early Christianity in Gloucestershire
by Michael Hare

The Roman Period

Christianity was first introduced into Gloucestershire at an unknown date during the Roman period, probably during the course of the 2nd or 3rd centuries. As a provincial capital Cirencester is likely to have been the seat of a Roman bishopric. It is indeed from Cirencester that our earliest Christian evidence is found, a piece of plaster with the Christian word-square SATOR AREPO scratched onto its surface (now in the Corinium Museum). This fragment probably belongs to the period when Christians were still persecuted.

After the Peace of the Church in AD. 312, Christianity became an official religion, though it was still not the faith of the majority of the population. From the 4th century our most substantial evidence is the existence of a number of stones inscribed with the chi-rho symbol at the major Roman villa of Chedworth; Christianity was evidently well-established at this villa in the late Roman period. To the evidence from Chedworth we can only add two possibly Christian lead tanks from Bourton-on-the-Water and a 4th century intaglio with a representation of the Good Shepherd found in recent excavations at the villa at Barnsley.

It will be seen that the archaeological evidence for Christianity in Roman Gloucestershire is meagre; what has been found comes exclusively from the Cotswolds. Pagan Roman and native British cults continued to flourish in the 4th century, and there were important temples at Uley in the Cotswolds and at Lydney in the Forest of Dean.

The Dark Ages

The 5th and 6th and first half of the 7th centuries are truly dark ages. At the moment it is impossible to ascertain how far pagan Roman and British cults continued or whether Christianity became the dominant religion. After the late 6th century we must also take into account the possible presence of the pagan Germanic traditions of the Anglo-Saxon invaders.

We can, however, draw some tentative conclusions. It is well-known that Christianity flourished on both sides of the Severn estuary in the 5th and 6th centuries. In the 6th century a distinctive form of Celtic Christianity developed in these areas, made famous by saints such as David, Illtud, Petroc and Samson. Christianity was firmly established in southern Wales, Cornwall, Devon and Somerset at the same time that eastern England was being overrun by Anglo-Saxon settlers.

In south-east Wales the principal saint was Dyfrig whose work certainly extended to the Wye valley. Recent research has shown that this early Welsh

Christianity extended into at least one part of our county, the southern end of the Forest of Dean. The *Book of Llandaff* provides documentary evidence for the existence of a Welsh monastery at Lancaut about 625, while at nearby Tidenham a Welsh church existed around the year 700. Both churches were probably founded at a much earlier date. A little further north, the place-name St. Briavel's indicates the probability of a foundation of the same period.

In the rest of the county the evidence is less tangible, but there is increasing evidence to suggest the presence of a sub-Roman British Christianity. Burials, probably Christian and dating from the 5th or 6th centuries, have been found beneath the churches at Frocester and at St. Mary de Lode in Gloucester. The evidence of the final phases of the Roman temple at Uley suggests that Christianity may have replaced the cult of Mercury. It may also be noted that 12th-century legends refer to a 5th century bishop of Gloucester called Eldad or Aldate, and it is possible that these legends have some historical basis. There was a medieval church (now destroyed) dedicated to St. Aldate in Gloucester. Recent studies therefore tend to indicate that British Christianity was the dominant religion in Gloucestershire in the 5th and 6th centuries, but the evidence is tentative and much more archaeological research is needed before firm conclusions can be drawn.

The pagan Anglo-Saxons began to settle on the Cotswolds during the 6th century and assumed political control of the lower Severn valley after the battle of Dyrham in 577 when the British kings of Gloucester, Cirencester and Bath were killed. However, it is improbable that the Anglo-Saxons were more than a ruling elite in the period after 577 and the influence of their religion was apparently slight. By contrast with eastern England where place-names provide ample evidence for pagan Germanic religion, there is not a single place-name of this character in Gloucestershire.

The establishment of Anglo-Saxon Christianity

In the 7th century Gloucestershire (except the forest of Dean) formed part of the kingdom of the Hwicce, which covered an area corresponding to the modern counties of north Avon, Gloucestershire, Worcestershire and south-west Warwickshire. We know from a casual comment made by the Venerable Bede, writing in the year 731, that Christianity was the established religion of both the rulers and people of the Hwicce in about 660. However, the creation in our area – and indeed throughout England – of a regular church along traditional Roman lines is an achievement to be attributed principally to Archbishop Theodore of Canterbury (669–690).

In 680, Archbishop Theodore established a cathedral church to serve the territory of the Hwicce at Worcester. During the course of the late 7th and 8th centuries 'minster' churches were founded throughout the diocese. These minster churches were served by a body of clergy responsible for the pastoral care of a wide area, sometimes up to 50 square miles in size. There were minster churches of particular importance at Gloucester (founded in about 681), Berkeley, Cirencester and Deerhurst.

There is little surviving architecture and sculpture from the 7th and 8th centuries. At Deerhurst the surviving Anglo-Saxon church is of quite exceptional complexity; at least six separate Saxon building phases have been identified and the earliest phases probably belong to this period. At Cirencester excavations north of the present parish church have revealed a major church built on a basilican plan, which in all probability is to be dated to the 7th or 8th centuries; no trace of this church is now visible above ground.

The Anglo-Saxons erected standing crosses at church sites and other holy places. Unfortunately none of these crosses have been preserved intact, but a number of interesting fragments survive. The largest and probably the earliest is the roadside cross at Lypiatt near Bisley, which may date from the late 7th century. Several fragments of 9th century crosses may be seen in Gloucester City Museum.

The late-Saxon period

The late-Saxon period saw major changes in the organisation of the Anglo-Saxon church. The Viking invasions of the late 9th century had left the English church in a parlous state, with literature and scholarship virtually non-existent. In the mid-10th century there was a religious revival which led to the establishment of monasteries organised along regular Benedictine lines; their importance in the history of the Anglo-Saxon church cannot be stressed too strongly.

In Gloucestershire there were three Benedictine monasteries in the late-Saxon period, Deerhurst, Gloucester St. Peter, and Winchcombe; all three were refoundations of former minster churches. Winchcombe (reformed about 972) was one of the major abbeys of late-Saxon England, but unfortunately both Winchcombe and Gloucester have left no visible traces. The complexity of the church at Deerhurst has already been mentioned, and it is likely that some parts of the present church (including the ornate polygonal apse) date from the Benedictine phase. St. Aelfheah, who became archbishop of Canterbury from 1005–1012 and was martyred by the Danes, began his monastic career as a young man at Deerhurst before 970.

A second major change in the late-Saxon period was the establishment of the parochial system. Between the 10th and 12th centuries the large minster parishes founded in the early days of Anglo-Saxon Christianity were broken up to form smaller parishes. Local thegns established churches to serve their estates, and the estate became the parish attached to the church. By the 12th century most villages had a church or at least a chapel of ease.

The foundation of one Gloucestershire parish church is recounted in the *Life of St Wulfstan*, who was bishop of Worcester from 1062–1096. The *Life* relates how Wulfstan was summoned to Longney (just south of Gloucester) to consecrate a church built by Ailsi, the local thegn. A dispute ensued over a tree in the churchyard, resolved by a miracle performed by Wulfstan; for the author of the *Life* the miracle was the point of the story, but for us it provides a practical illustration of the way in which local churches were founded.

A substantial quantity of architecture and sculpture still survives from late-Saxon Gloucestershire. Many of the old minster churches retained their importance at this time and were rebuilt on a substantial scale. Bibury, where there are traces of a Saxon rood above the chancel-arch, is a good example. Part of the 'new minster' of St. Oswald in Gloucester, founded around 900 to serve the royal palace, survives as a standing ruin. There are also substantial remains of smaller parish churches; among the most noteworthy survivals are Coln Rogers, Daglingworth and Duntisbourne Rouse. These churches, together with other more fragmentary examples, display the full repertoire of the idiosyncratic features of Anglo-Saxon architecture such as long-and-short quoining, jambs and arches built of through-stones, pilaster-strips, square hood-mouldings, triangular-headed doorways and the like.

The sculpture of the late Saxon period shows a much greater variety than the crosses of the early period. In addition to crosses, we find grave-covers, figure sculpture including several Crucifixions, and architectural sculpture such as carved capitals, decorated string-courses and imposts, beast-head stops and sundials. There is a major collection of architectural sculpture *in situ* at Deerhurst. Other important sites include Daglingworth (with several figure sculptures) and Wormington (with a large Crucifixion). The minster churches at Berkeley, Bibury and Bisley have all produced a number of fragments (though most of the Berkeley pieces are not on display and much of the Bibury sculpture is in the British Museum).

Two pieces of outstanding merit must be specially mentioned, as they are of national rather than local importance. The first is an early 10th century grave-cover carved with foliage found in recent excavations at St. Oswald's, Gloucester and now on display in the City Museum; the second is an 11th century relief carving of Christ in Majesty set in the south wall of the tower at Beverstone.

The distribution of the surviving Anglo-Saxon architecture and sculpture of Gloucestershire is of interest. There is a marked concentration in the southern Cotswolds; well over half the sites with Saxon material in the county fall within a ten-mile radius of Cirencester. By contrast there is an almost total absence of Anglo-Saxon work in the northern Cotswolds, probably for reasons of land-ownership too complex for discussion in this brief note. In the area between the Cotswold scarp and the River Severn, there is little surviving Anglo-Saxon work except at major churches such as Deerhurst, Gloucester and Berkeley. To the west of the river Severn, the only surviving evidence is provided by two sculptures from Newent, probably the principal settlement in north-west Gloucestershire in the Anglo-Saxon period.

This distribution reflects both the geology of the county and the pattern of settlement. The Cotswolds provide the best stone for building and carving; they were also the most densely settled and prosperous area of the county. Away from the Cotswolds suitable stone was not locally available and only the richer churches could afford to build or carve in stone. In the Vales of Berkeley and Gloucester and in west Gloucestershire, it is likely that wood was the material used in most Anglo-Saxon churches.

The Church of England Churches
by David Verey

The Normans

None of the Saxons' wooden churches have survived in Gloucestershire; but some of the Normans' decorative motifs, such as the beast's head stops to a stone hood-moulding over a doorway or arch, may be a revival of the decoration on a wooden church or on the prow of a Viking ship. Our stone churches, however, go back for a thousand years. They have survived far better than domestic buildings, and the reason is that most men were still living in mud hovels when they built stone churches. They should be the concern of us all, whether we are members of the Church of England or not, because they enshrine our history and our heritage. Members of the Church wish to see that they continue to be used as they always have, for worship. It is the saddest possible thing for an ancient church to become redundant.

There is no easily defined line to be drawn between Anglo-Saxon and Norman architecture. It used to be said that herring-bone masonry was pre-Conquest; but that theory is now discounted. 'Long and short' work in the quoins of buildings, and the use of megalithic stones, however, are usually signs of a building-date before 1066.

Gloucestershire is one of the richest counties in respect of surviving Norman architecture. On the grandest scale we have Gloucester Cathedral and Tewkesbury Abbey, where the almost exact comparison, even to dimensions, of the tall cylindrical piers and short arches of the nave arcades clearly points to local fashion and imitation. Men of outstanding quality were brought from Normandy to fill high offices in the Church, like Serlo the first Norman abbot of St. Peter's Abbey, Gloucester. William the Conqueror kept court at Christmas in Gloucester, and he ordered the Domesday survey when he was there. Several of the Cotswold manors were given to William and Matilda's own monasteries at Caen, such as Minchinhampton which belonged to the Abbaye aux Dames right up to 1415.

Gloucestershire was in the Diocese of Worcester and we know that the Bishop Wulfstan urged on the lords of the manors the duty of building churches. There were also a number of monasteries which have unfortunately not survived the Dissolution: Cirencester, Winchcombe and Hailes. This is all the more tragic because there are no records of what they were like, and so we can only guess what riches of architecture and sculpture were deliberately destroyed. Several of the churches round Cirencester – South Cerney, Siddington, Elkstone. Quenington, Eastleach and Windrush – show signs of a regional school of sculpture, perhaps centred on Cirencester Abbey though this cannot be substantiated. The beakhead ornaments round the soffits and jambs of the elaborately carved doorways have parallels in Normandy which have survived to this day. Their date is mid-12th century, so the troubled reign of King Stephen does not seem to have interfered with church building.

South door of Elkstone church
Samuel Lysons, 1794.

Door of South Cerney Church
Samuel Lysons, 1794.

Door of Siddington church   *Samuel Lysons, 1794.*

Windrush has two complete orders of beakheads, the outer over the arch and attached shafts, the inner continuous over the roll mouldings and jambs; all are beakheads with almond-shaped eyes, except possibly four or five, and resemble the almond-shaped eyes of the beasts at Saxon Deerhurst.

During the second half of the 12th Century the Virgin was much venerated. The South doorway at Quenington contains a tympanum of the Coronation of the Virgin. It is one of the earliest examples of this subject to have survived.

The sublimest work of the 12th Century is, however, the Head and Foot of a wooden Crucifix, found at South Cerney, and which, it is now suggested, may in fact be Spanish, and have been brought back from Compostela by a pilgrim. Of local stone sculpture it most nearly resembles a capital at Leonard Stanley, which is the closest thing in Gloucestershire to the Herefordshire 'school' and its known connections with Santiago de Compostela.

Another treasure of the Cotswold churches is the font at Southrop. Its probable date is c. 1180, but the figures are sculptured with far greater freedom than those on the font at Rendcomb. There are eight arches with five armoured women representing the Virtues, the other three being Moses, Ecclesia and Synagogue, indicating a considerable degree of iconographical sophistication. The Virtues trample on their opposite Vices, their names incised on the arches with the Vices' names written backwards on the panels, i.e. Patience on Ira, Modestia on Ebrietas, Misericordia on Invidia, Temperancia on Luxuria, and Largitas on Avaricia. What could be more instructive or more civilized?

Early English and Decorated Architecture

Many Gloucestershire churches were built within a hundred years of the Norman Conquest. Architectural evidence of this can be seen all round. Compared with this, and the last medieval building period which we call Perpendicular, the intervening 13th and 14th centuries, stylistically known as the Early English and Decorated periods, have not left so great an impression in Gloucestershire.

The 13th century was a time when the clergy were undergoing a revival of asceticism and wished to set up a more emphatic distinction between themselves and the laity. The consequence was a general lengthening of chancels, thus creating a new east wall, generally with three lancet windows for the Trinity. Many instances of this treatment can be seen. When we remember that the chancel was divided from the nave by the rood screen, the separation of the clergy in their more spacious chancels, and the laity in the nave, would have been complete. Most examples, however, are on the more peaceful Cotswolds, the west part of Gloucestershire suffered from border warfare. Examples are at Wyck Rissington, Cherington, Bibury, Eastleach Turville, Shipton Oliffe, Icomb, Meysey Hampton, and Little Rissington. This form of chancel survived in the 19th century as it found favour with the High Church movement; but it is sometimes an embarrassment with the modern liturgical movement today. Three churches outside the Cotswolds, however, have outstanding 13th century features. Berkeley has a west end influenced by Bristol fashion, Slimbridge a splendid nave, and Teddington has late 13th century work moved from Hailes Abbey at the Dissolution.

The Decorated style is hardly represented on the Cotswolds at all, except that at Longborough there is a fine 14th century south transept, and another at Minchinhampton and Todenham is almost wholly 14th century. Ballflower decoration is found in the west. The windows in the north aisle at Badgeworth are very similar to the Decorated windows in the south aisle of Gloucester Cathedral, c. 1318, all profusely enriched with ballflower. This was also the period for spire-building and most of the churches at the bottom of the escarpment seem to have spires, Standish, Slimbridge, Stone, Haresfield, the parish church at Cheltenham, Leckhampton and Shurdington. And there are good 14th century spires at Ruardean, Westbury-on-Severn and Stroud. Painswick spire is later.

Perpendicular and Tudor

The final phases of medieval English church building are known as Perpendicular (from the middle of the 14th century to the end of the 15th century) and Tudor (the beginning of the 16th century). The great Perpendicular churches on the Cotswolds are often called 'wool' churches and are some of the most notable in the county, particularly those at Cirencester, Northleach, Chipping Campden, Fairford, Winchcombe, Lechlade, Chedworth, and Rendcomb. The aim of the builders was to obtain more space and light. In many existing churches the nave was rebuilt much taller and lit by clerestory windows. The effect was as if some great college chapel had been dropped into the middle of the parish church. It also meant that a window could be introduced high above the chancel arch, a distinctive local feature in the Cotswolds. The clerestory windows are often close together with the very flat arches daringly constructed to obtain as much glass and therefore light as possible.

The colour of the Cotswold oolitic stone, shades from yellow, through cream to deep brown. The variations in colour are due to an iron mineral in the rock which makes it a richer colour such as the yellow Guiting stone. It also grows lichens, deep orange, a light buff, blue grey and pure silver, a diffusion of yellow, red and violet in the sunlight.

The mid-15th century tower at St. Peter's Abbey, Gloucester, was influential, and splendid Perpendicular towers were built at Chipping Campden, Northleach, and the other 'wool' churches and at Coates, Coberley, Compton Abdale, Elmstone-Hardwicke, Leigh, Kempsford, Oxenton, Gloucester St. Nicholas, St. Mary de Crypt, Wotton-under-Edge, and elsewhere. It was also the age of the chantry chapel, where priests were paid to say masses for the souls of the departed. A good surviving example is the Garstang chapel at Cirencester with its altar in the nave and surrounded by an elaborately carved screen. At the Reformation the chantries were suppressed and their endowments confiscated.

Just before the Reformation the style may be called Tudor. Various influences were introduced from abroad, particularly Spanish. Domed polygonal turrets to be seen on Henry VII's chapel at Westminster or Christchurch tower, Oxford, had their echo at Chipping Campden on the pentice stair-turret, and at other places.

Post-Reformation

Post-Reformation churches, or church alterations hardly exist in Gloucestershire before the reign of Queen Anne. There was, however, a great deal of alteration to church furnishings to suit the new liturgies. Jacobean pulpits abound. Archbishop Laud (a Dean of Gloucester) introduced altar rails. Fonts went out with Oliver Cromwell and came back with Charles II, though not always the originals. In the 18th century some towers had to be rebuilt, and probably more was done than we imagine, owing to the change of taste which came about in the 19th century making all things Georgian unfashionable and therefore reversible. The little church at Hawling still retains its Georgian Venetian window at the east end, and there is a similar window at Temple Guiting in the transept. History marches on, and the Oxford Movement decreed that windows should return to their original and more ecclesiastical appearance. Georgian innovations hardly ever survived Victorian restorations.

The Nineteenth Century

The Anglo-Catholic revival was felt most strongly in Gloucestershire through John Keble and his brother Thomas who was vicar of Bisley, where Anglo-Catholicism has to be associated with the cause of the workers. The weavers in the Bisley area suffered greatly in the first half of the 19th century from lack of work. Tom Keble built churches at Bussage, France Lynch and Oakridge. 19th century churches were built throughout the Forest of Dean. Medieval churches survive all round the perimeter; but they did not exist inside the Forest before.

In 1838 we learn from the Rev. F.E. Witt's Diary that the Gloucester Diocesan Church Building Association held a meeting with regard to the archdeaconry of Gloucester, at which aid was agreed for various churches to be built or enlarged. The enlargement of Horsley was decided on, and a new church in Leckhampton parish, and another contiguous to Gloucester in the parish of Hempsted. This latter refers to St. Luke's opened in 1841. St. Stephen's was built to replace it and was originally called St. Luke's. The Leckhampton church was also rebuilt later in the 19th century, and is now St. Philip and St. James built in 1870. Gloucestershire has its share of the vast numbers of churches built in England in the 19th century, but not so many as in more industrial places. Although nearly all medieval churches were restored – sometimes drastically – in the 19th century, the balance of the responsibility left us is heavily on the medieval side, about the merit of which there can be no argument. There are, however, some outstandingly interesting 19th Century churches such as Gambier-Parry's masterpiece at Highnam or the local architect, Francis Niblett's church at Fretherne, and John Middleton's five churches in Cheltenham and another at Clearwell.

Roman Catholics
by David Verey

It would not appear that Gloucestershire had so many recusants as the neighbouring counties of Worcestershire and Warwickshire. Although there are claims that Lypiatt Park was connected with the Gunpowder Plot, most of those involved fled to their homes further west.

The Norman church of St. James at Postlip belongs to the Roman Catholics today; but this combination is unique. The chapel at Prinknash Park is owned by the Benedictine monks of Prinknash Abbey. Part of it is early 16th century. A boss taken from the house has the emblems of Edward IV and there is 16th century stained glass.

In 1845 William Leigh, who had just been converted to the Roman Catholic faith, bought the Woodchester Park estate, and proceeded to build a Dominican Priory of which only the Church of Our Lady of the Annunciation survives. The church at the neighbouring Franciscan Convent is also in use. Both were designed by Charles Hansom. In nearby Stroud the Convent of St. Rose of Lima was built in 1867 by Benjamin Bucknall, Leigh's architect at Woodchester Park, (where there is also a chapel,) and the friend and translator of Viollet-le-Duc. At St. Rose's the chapel is used; and the Church of Our Lady of the Immaculate Conception (1858 by C.A. Buckler) is close by. At Painswick there is a church built in Friday Street by Peter Falconer in c. 1950, with a pretty cupola.

Both Gloucester and Cheltenham have eye-catching churches with tall spires.

Charles Hansom's model of Woodchester Priory with church, 1846.

Nonconformist Meeting-Houses and Chapels
by Philip Hayden

During the 17th century the Presbyterians, Independents, Baptists, Quakers and the Unitarians all established churches in Gloucestershire. The Presbyterians, however, were never strong in the county and none of their buildings have survived. Only in one or two places did the Unitarians sustain a congregation and only the building at Cirencester has been preserved. A number of Quaker meeting-houses were built before 1740 but the subsequent decline of that denomination has meant that all but four buildings have been demolished. Most of the early meeting-houses of the Baptists and Independents have also been lost, though the Baptist meeting-house at Tewkesbury (c. 1695) has undergone restoration and the Independent one at Cam (c. 1702) survives.

The importance of the Evangelical Revival to Gloucestershire, and especially the influence of George Whitefield and the Calvinistic Methodists, more so than John Wesley, cannot be underestimated; but Whitefield's regional headquarters at Rodborough was rebuilt in 1837, while of those Independent congregations which welcomed him and his preachers only the meeting-houses at Painswick (rebuilt 1803) and Dursley (rebuilt 1808) still survive. Similarly, the chapels at Birdwood (1814) and Cheltenham (1816) remain as the only witnesses to the involvement of the Countess of Huntingdon in the county. Rowland Hill's leadership of Independent and Calvanistic churches in Gloucestershire after Whitefield's death, and his efforts to erect chapels may, however, be forgotten for none of these buildings survive whilst his own Tabernacle at Wotton-under-Edge (rebuilt 1898) has been refurbished as a museum. During the same period the Arminian, or Wesleyan, Methodists were not unsuccessful; but only Stroud (built 1763 and now used by the Salvation Army) and Painswick (built 1806 and taken over by Baptists in 1831) give any indication of early Methodist preaching-houses. The Independents were able to erect a number of completely new meeting-houses, and replace small decaying ones during the latter part of the 18th century. The greatest effect of the Revival was on Gloucestershire Baptists who, through the efforts of the churches at Horsley and Bourton-on-the-Water, experienced remarkable growth. Many new meeting-houses were erected and a number rebuilt; but, like the Independents, most surviving examples date from the first decades of the 19th century.

The majority of these meeting-houses were built of Cotswold stone, though in the north and south-west a number were constructed of brick and sometimes faced with ashlar or plaster. None of the interiors of the surviving 18th century meeting-houses have remained intact, and only a few contain pulpits or galleries which give an indication of their restrained, simple design; a characteristic derived both from many Nonconformists' convictions that outward ornament was immodest, and their desire to avoid unnecessary expenditure. However a growing awareness and rising confidence in Nonconformist taste is indicated by the more elaborate external detailing, and the use of porches and porticos and more ornamental fittings towards the close of the 18th century. Some even went so far as to include "Gothick" details. Nonconformists were no longer relying on voluntary labour, and the skill of local masons and carpenters, or simply adapting buildings in a vernacular tradition.

A number of churches employed provincial architects and builders though the Independent meeting-house at Kingswood (rebuilt 1821) was designed by it's minister, Charles Daniell. Most chapels followed the classical tradition during the Georgian period, but both the Greek and Gothic Revivals found some expression in the Nonconformist architecture of Gloucestershire. Although no large-scale temples were built, many chapels used Neo-classical elements, the Baptist chapel at Cinderford (1843) having full-height Corinthian pilasters and an entablature. The following year the Salem Baptist chapel at Cheltenham was constructed in the Gothic style. Although a number of chapels were "gothicised" in later years, the style was not popular in the county. Indeed, Painswick Independents rejected Joseph Tait's design of 1886, not only because of it's "Anglican" tower but also because of it's cost. A considerable number of chapels, of all denominations, were built, or rebuilt, in varying styles – Italianate, Venetian and Romanesque – during the Victorian period by both local designers and, in some cases, by architects who specialised in chapel-building bequeathing Gloucestershire an excellent library of Nonconformist architecture.

During the 20th century, due to the migration of many people, failing attendances and the merging of congregations, a large number of Nonconformist places of worship have become redundant and been demolished. It is now imperative to preserve those of architectural and historical importance.

Ampney Crucis. The gabled head of the 15th century churchyard Cross showing the Crucifixion with St. John and the Virgin (on the other sides are the Virgin, St. Laurence with his gridiron, and a man in armour of c. 1415.) It was found walled up inside the entrance to the rood loft, and restored in c. 1860.

P.D. Turner.

Above **Ampney St. Peter.** Low western tower at the end of an 11th century nave. *David Vine courtesy Corinium Museum*

Right **Baunton.** 14th Century wall-painting of St. Christopher, with green and brown fish swimming around in the stream through which he is carrying the Christ Child. *P.D. Turner*

Above **Berkeley.** The mid–13th-century west end of the nave has five graduated round-headed lanc windows. Below are three pointed arches with steep gables and a cusped miner arch over the doorwa Bristol fashion. The detached tower was rebuilt in 1750. *E. Gethyn-Jone*

Below **Cheltenham, Christ Church.** 1838–40, designed in the Gothic style for the frequenters of summer resort, where 'great spiritual advantages' were to be had as well as purgative waters.
Robert Paterson Collection, courtesy Gloucestershire Record Office. Slide No 10 10C

Above **Cirencester.** The Church of St. John the Baptist seen from the east. *Clive Friend, courtesy Woodmansterne Ltd.*

Below **Cirencester.** The Bridges tomb, c. 1620, in the east end of the Lady Chapel. *Clive Friend, courtesy Woodmansterne Ltd.*

Above **Coleford.** Independent Chapel, now United Reformed Church, 1804. Rebuilt 1842. *P. Hayden.*

Left **Cirencester.** The great Tudor nave, 1516–30, brilliantly inserted into the existing church and rising much higher than its predecessor, with an almost continuous clerestory row of four-light windows including the great window over the chancel arch, a local characteristic.

Nicholas Servian, courtesy Woodmansterne Ltd.

Below **Colesbourne.** A medieval church in Mr. Elwes's park. *B. Waters.*

Coln Rogers. Anglo–Saxon church which has survived almost intact except for the rebuilding of the east end of the chancel, and the tower. *Chris Bowler, courtesy Corinium Museum.*

Coln St. Aldwyns. Appropriated to the abbey of Gloucester from 1217 to the Dissolution, the tower has late Norman and Early English lower stages with the upper stage built during the time of Abbot John Gamage c. 1284. A Perpendicular top has crocketed pinnacles and a pierced parapet. *B. Waters.*

Daylesford. The church was rebuilt in 1860 and has good stained glass by Clayton & Bell, with small-scale scenes illustrating the life of St. Paul.

P. D. Turner.

Deerhurst. The Priory church is an Anglo-Saxon monument of the first order. A monastery existed here in 804, and the building partly dates from this period.   *P.D. Turner.*

Above **Down Ampney.** Transitional Norman arcades painted with 13th century red cinqufoil flow and an elaborate late 19th century rood screen. *P.D. Tu*

Below **Duntisbourne Rouse.** Anglo-Saxon and Norman. The sloping site has been used to mak small crypt chapel below the chancel. *P.D. Tu*

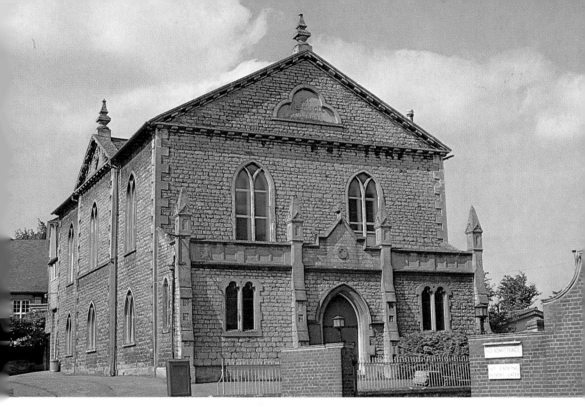

Above **Dursley.** Tabernacle. Now United Reformed Church. Non-conformist 'fearless confidence' galleried meeting house. Founded by Independents 1715, rebuilt for Whitefieldites 1764; rebuilt with minister's house 1807–9; completely restored in 1880's when the original central doorway was moved to the south end and a porch added.   *P. Hayden.*

Below **Elkstone.** In a district rich in Norman churches, this is the most interesting and best preserved, and there is a rare stone vault in the sanctuary.   *B. Waters.*

Above **Elmore.** The churchyard contains one of the finest table-tombs in the county, and seve[r]
others nearly as good. Painswick stone suitable for deep undercutting is used with Minchinhampt[on]
stone tops, even though Elmore is in the Vale. The Church is mainly Early English.

P.D. Turn[er]

Below **Fairford.** Late Perpendicular church c. 1480–1500, famous for its complete survival [of]
contemporary stained glass.

B. Wate[rs]

Farmcote. A tiny church with attractive furnishings, a 16th century monument and a 17th century pulpit.

P.D. Turner.

Gloucester, St. Mary de Crypt. Rich Perpendicular carving in the chancel, perhaps made for Henry
Dene, Prior of Lanthony and afterwards Archbishop of Canterbury. *P.D. Turner*

Gloucester, St. Mary de Lode. Norman arch leading to the chancel and supporting the central tower.

P.D. Turner.

Above **Hampnett.** Small Norman church, in which, as at Elkstone, the vaulting in the sanctua
survives and here painted by the Victorian incumbent, c. 1871. *Chris Bowler, courtesy Corinium Museu*

Below **Hewelsfield.** Norman church on the edge of the Forest of Dean near the watershed between t
rivers Severn and Wye. The circular churchyard indicates great antiquity. *David W. Pric*

Highnam. The Church is a Victorian masterpiece by Henry Woodyer and Thomas Gambier-Parry. The stained glass on the south is particularly notable, designed by Pugin and made by Hardman: the Nativity. *P.D. Turner.*

Kempley, St. Edward. 1903, a personification of the Arts and Crafts Movement by Lethaby's clerk-of-works, the twenty-five year old Randall Wells, who was given a free hand by the patron Lord Beauchamp.

P.D. Turner.

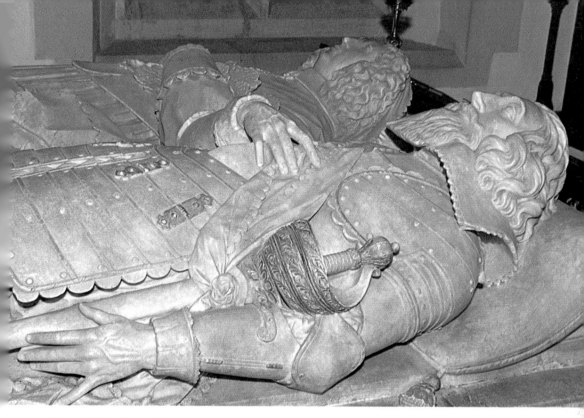

Above **Miserden.** The Derbyshire alabaster effigies of Sir William and Lady Sandys c. 1644, in an over-restored but originally Saxon church. *P.D. Turner.*

Below **North Cerney.** Exquisitely preserved church of all periods. Note the outside steps and door to the gallery. *B. Walters.*

Northleach The South porch (c. 1400) of one of the great "wool" churches of the Cotswolds, on which four medieval images have survived, together with crocketed pinnacles and a stair-turret to the upper chamber.   *D. Verey.*

Above **Oddington,** St. Nicholas. 13th century tower built on the east end of the south aisle, with a 15th century top stage which has lost its pinnacles. The church escaped 19th century alterations and retains its wall-paintings. The bells have been rehung for ringing. *B. Waters.*

Left **Painswick.** A unique and most splendid collection of table-tombs in any churchyard. "Tea-caddies", a Painswick name, can be concave-sided, octagonal or cylindrical with lids. The large church has a famous spire. *P.D. Turner.*

Rodmarton. Another church with a pretty 14th century tower and spire, and well kept churchyard.
P.D. Turner.

Above **Quenington.** The North doorway is a mid 12th-century work of great richness and splendour. The innter arch has chevrons at right angles, further out is a band of limpet shells. The abaci are carved with star, cable, knot and billet mouldings, and the capitals with jacks-in-the green symbols of fertility. The tympanum shows the Harrowing of Hell. The subject in the South porch is the Coronation of the Virgin. *D. Verey.*

Below **Standish.** The churchyard has a good collection of 17th and 18th century gravestones, and a beautiful church as well. *P.D. Turner.*

Left **South Cerney.** The Head of Christ from the former rood, perhaps mid–12th-century Spanish work brought back by a pilgrim from Compostela. Many other delights in this church.

P.D. Turner

Below **Saintbury.** In a fine setting on the edge of the Cotswold escarpment. Norman church with 14th century tower and spire.

David Viner, courtesy Corinium Museum

Southrop. The Font of Southrop. The Virtues trample on their opposite Vices, their names incised on the arches with the Vices written backwards on the panels. In the spandrels of the arches are the Heavenly mansions. Here Modestia (moderation) overcomes Ebrietas (excess). *P.D. Turner*

Stanton. Late Norman to Perpendicular, with notable furnishings by Sir Ninian Comper. The Perpendicular south aisle and porch were added when a possession of Winchcombe Abbey. *B. Waters.*

Above **Teddington.** Early Norman chancel arch. The large Royal Arms are those of William and Mary, 1689, painted on the wall-plaster. *D.Verey.*

Below **Tetbury.** Splendid late 18th Century Gothic church, more elegant than archaeologically correct, with windows of amazing size. The tower and spire were rebuilt in 1890. *Peter A. Harding.*

Tewkesbury. The great Norman tower, from the North-East.

Howard C. Moore courtesy Woodmansterne Lt

Tewkesbury. The nave showing the cylindrical columns and round capitals, probably complete at the time of the consecration in 1121, a regional characteristic, and to be compared with Gloucester Cathedral.   *Malcolm E. Osman. courtesy Woodmansterne Ltd.*

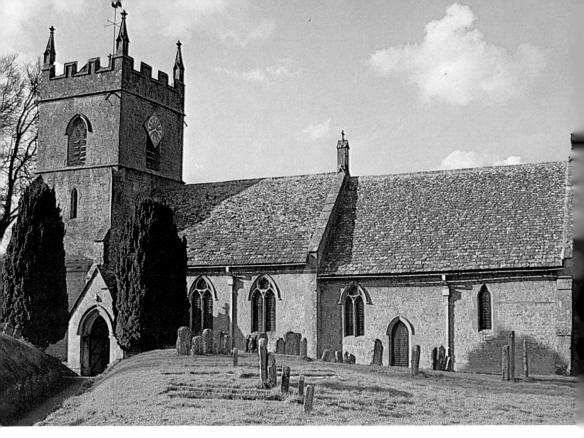

Above **Upper Slaughter.** Originally Norman; but the later insertion of a rib-vaulted tower in the west bay of the nave, (rebuilt in its upper stages in the early 15th century,) caused dispersal of some of the Norman features in the church. In 1854 a mortuary chapel was added by public subscription over the grave of the Rev. Francis Witts.   *P.D. Turner.*

Below **Withington.** Norman church with elegant Perpendicular additions, on a very ancient site.
                                                                                                P.D. Turner.

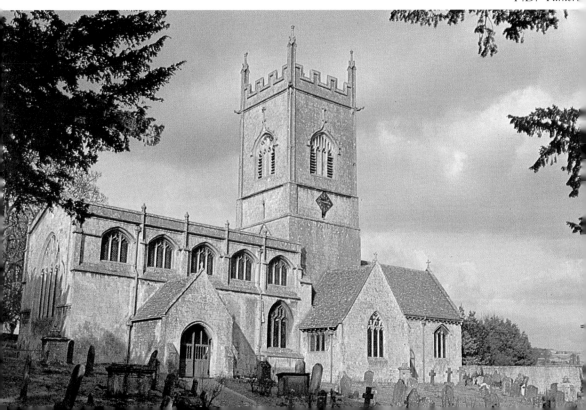

The Gloucestershire Historic Churches Preservation Trust.

Established in 1980 the Trust is an autonomous body whose aim is to help Parochial Church Councils cover the cost of church repairs. It is a voluntary organisation entirely dependent upon public donations for its well being. Under the terms of its Constitution it may make grants for the preservation of any church, chapel, or any other building used for worship for the time being, whether belonging to the Church of England or any other religious body or possessing notable architectural features or historical associations within Gloucestershire. The term 'historical' does not necessarily have any connotation of date. The Trust is a Registered Charity.

The organisation consists of an Executive council whose Members are drawn from each of sixteen Deanaries and is headed by two non-executive Joint Presidents and a number of Vice Presidents. The Lord Lieutenant of Gloucestershire and the Right Rev. Lord Bishop of Gloucester are the Trust's present Joint Presidents.

> For further details please apply
> The Secretary,
> G.H.C.P.T. PO Box No 8
> Cirencester, Glos.
> GL7 1SZ

All donations whether large or small are welcome.

Church of England Churches

Note: C = century, i.e. C14 = 14th Century. c = circa,
EE = Early English: Dec = Decorated: Perp = Perpendicular.

ABENHALL, St. Michael. Medieval. C14 and 15. Free miners' heraldry.

ADLESTROP, St. Mary Magdalene, Medieval, restored in C18 probably by Sanderson Miller, and again in early 1860s.

ALDERLEY, St. Kenelm. Perp West tower, otherwise c. 1802. Monuments.

ALDERTON, St. Margaret, Mostly C14, with Perp tower. Restored c. 1890.

ALDSWORTH, St. Bartholomew. Medieval. Norman, and Perp North aisle c. 1500.

ALSTONE, St. Margaret. Norman, Perp and C17. Restored in 1880, scraped.

ALVINGTON, St. Andrew. Medieval, drastically restored in C19.

AMBERLEY, Holy Trinity. 1836, by Robert Stokes of Cheltenham.

AMPNEY CRUCIS, Holy Rood. Saxon, Norman and medieval, with C19 restoration. Monuments. Churchyard Cross.

AMPNEY ST. MARY, St. Mary. Early C12, EE chancel, stone screen, wall paintings.

AMPNEY ST. PETER, St. Peter. Saxon, Norman. Restoration and additions probably by G.G. Scott, junior.

APPERLEY, Holy Trinity. 1856 by F.C. Penrose.

ARLINGHAM, St. Mary. Medieval, restored in C19, Furnishings. Stained glass Monuments.

ASHCHURCH, St. Nicholas. Norman, and medieval. Rood screen.

ASHLEWORTH, St. Andrew and St. Bartholomew. Norman and medieval. North transept C19.

ASHLEY, St. James. Norman. C19 chancel.

ASTON BLANK, St. Andrew. Norman, Perp tower.

ASTON-SUB-EDGE, St. Andrew. 1797 by Thomas Johnson of Warwick.

AVENING, Holy Cross. Norman. Cruciform and central tower. East window and South vestry restored in c. 1887. Monuments.

AWRE, St. Andrew. Norman, and Perp tower. EE chancel. Considerably unaltered.

AYLBURTON, St. Mary. Rebuilt on new site in 1856.

BADGEWORTH, Holy Trinity. Outstanding Dec North aisle. Chancel C19.

BAGENDON, St. Margaret. Saxon origin, Norman. Chancel rebuilt 1460–70. Stained glass.

BARNSLEY, St. Mary. Norman origin. Perp North aisle and tower with Jacobean parapet. Restored 1843–7.

BARNWOOD, St. Lawrence. Norman. Chancel rebuilt 1874–8. Perp West tower, and North chapel. C14 bellcote.

The **BARRINGTONS. GREAT BARRINGTON,** St. Mary. Norman, medieval and Tudor. Monuments.

LITTLE BARRINGTON, St. Peter. Norman and medieval.

BATSFORD, St. Mary. Rebuilt in 1861–2 in Neo-Norman style.

BAUNTON, St. Mary Magdalene. Norman and medieval. Wall painting.

BEACHLEY, St. John. 1833 by Foster and Okeley.

BENTHAM, St. Peter. 1888 by Sidney Gambier-Parry.

BERKELEY, St. Mary. Norman and medieval. C18 detached tower. Berkeley family chapel. Monuments. Wall paintings.

BERRY HILL, Christchurch. 1816.

BEVERSTON, St. Mary. Pre-Conquest sculpture. Norman and medieval. Restored in 1844 and 1901.

BIBURY, St. Mary. Saxon, Norman and medieval. Restored by Sir Gilbert Scott, 1863.

BIRDLIP, St. Mary. 1957 by H. Stratton Davis.

BISHOPS CLEEVE, St. Michael. Norman and medieval. Large Dec chancel. Restored C19. Central tower. Jacobean musicians' gallery. Monuments.

BISLEY, All Saints. Medieval. Restored 1862 by Rev. W.H. Lowder. West tower with spire.

BLAISDON, St. Michael. 1967 by F.R. Kempson.

BLEDINGTON, St. Leonard. Norman, medieval and outstanding Perp work. Stained glass.

BLOCKLEY, St. Peter & St. Paul. Norman, and C17, with C18 tower. Monuments.

BODDINGTON, St. Mary Magdalene. Norman and medieval. Restored 1876. Scraped.

BOURTON-ON-THE-HILL, St. Lawrence. Norman and medieval.

BOURTON-ON-THE-WATER, St. Lawrence. C18 tower, medieval chancel, the rest C19 by Sir T.G. Jackson.

BOX, St. Barnabas. 1953 by Peter Falconer.

BOXWELL, St. Mary. Medieval. C13 bellcote.

BREAM, St. James. 1823 by Rev. H. Poole. Altered 1860 by William White.

BRIMPSFIELD, St. Michael. Norman and medieval. Central tower.

BRIMSCOMBE, Holy Trinity. 1840.

BROADWELL, St. Paul. Norman and medieval. Restored 1860s.

BROCKWORTH, St. George. Norman, and medieval.

BROMSBERROW, St. Mary. Medieval. C18 chapel. C19 timber framed belfry and spire, and restorations.

BROOKTHORPE, St. Swithin. Medieval with C19 North aisle.

BUCKLAND, St. Michael. Medieval. C17 furnishings. Stained glass.

BULLEY, St. Michael. Norman, chancel rebuilt 1886.

BUSSAGE, St. Michael 1846 by J.P. Harrison. South aisle 1854 by G.F. Bodley.

CAINSCROSS, St. Matthew. 1835–7 by Charles Baker. Chancel 1898 by Walter Planck.

CAM. LOWER CAM, St. Bartholomew. 1844 by Rev. G. Madan.

UPPER CAM, St. George. Medieval. Chancel 1845.

CERNEY WICK, Holy Trinity. 1847 by J.P. St. Aubyn.

CHACELY, St. John the Baptist. Norman and medieval. Restored 1882 by E. Christian.

CHALFORD, Christ Church. 1724. Chancel added 1841 and altered 1857. Arts and Crafts furnishings.

CHARLTON ABBOTS, St. Martin. Rebuilt and restored in C19.

CHALRTON KINGS, St. Mary. Perp central tower. Mostly rebuilt 1877–8. Holy Apostles. 1871 by John Middleton.

CHEDWORTH, St. Andrew. Norman and Perp.

CHERINGTON, St. Nicholas. Medieval. EE Chancel.

CHELTENHAM, St. Mary. Parish church and only medieval church in town.
>Christ Church. 1838–4 by the Jearrads. Remodelled 1888–93 by J.H. Middleton.
>Emmanuel. 1936 by H. Rainger.
>St. Luke. 1854. Enlarged 1866 by John Middleton.
>St. Mark. 1862–7 by John Middleton.
>St. Matthew. 1878–9 by E. Christian.
>St. Paul. 1827–31 by J. Forbes.
>St. Peter. 1847–9 by S.W. Daukes.
>St. Stephen. 1873 by John Middleton.
>Holy Trinity. 1820–3 by G.A. Underwood.

CHIPPING CAMPDEN, St. James. Great Perp 'wool' church transformed in the C15 into a complete unity. Monuments.

CHURCHAM, St. Andrew. Norman, much rebuilt in 1878 by Waller & Son.

CHURCHDOWN, St. Bartholomew. Norman and medieval. Restored in 1880 by E. Christian.
>St. Andrew. 1903 by W.B. Wood.
>St. John. 1957 by D.I. Stratton Davis.

CINDERFORD, St. John. 1844 by E. Blore.
>St. Stephen. 1890, chancel 1893 by E.H. Lingen Barker.
>St. Michael, Soudley. 1910.

CIRENCESTER, St. John the Baptist. The largest of the great Perp 'wool' churches, otherwise Norman and medieval. Tower c. 1400. Restored by Sir Gilbert Scott 1865–7. Monuments.
>Holy Trinity, Watermoor. 1850–1, by Sir Gilbert Scott.

CLAPTON-ON-THE-HILL, St. James. Small late C12 church.

CLEARWELL, St. Peter. 1866, by John Middleton.

CLEEVE HILL, St. Peter. 1907 by E.D. Hoyland.

CLIFFORD'S MESNE, St. Peter. 1882 by E.S. Harris.

COALEY, St. Bartholomew. Perp tower otherwise rebuilt 1854–8 by Jacques & Son.

COATES, St. Matthew. Norman and medieval. Perp tower.

COBERLEY, St. Giles. Perp tower, South chapel c. 1340. Nave rebuilt 1869–72 by John Middleton. Monuments.

COLEFORD, St. John. 1880 by F.S. Waller.

COLESBOURNE, St. James. Norman and medieval; cruciform. Restored 1851–2 by D. Brandon.

COLN ROGERS, St. Andrew. Anglo-Saxon.

COLN ST. ALDWYNS, St. John the Baptist. Norman and medieval.

COLN ST. DENNIS, St. James. Norman chancel, nave and central tower.

COMPTON ABDALE, St. Oswald. Medieval; Perp tower. Restored 1883 by E. Christian and in 1904–5.

CONDICOTE, St. Nicholas. Norman and medieval. Restored 1888.

CORSE, St. Margaret. Norman and C14.

COWLEY, St. Mary. c. 1200. Restored 1872. Perp tower.

CRANHAM, St. James. Mainly C15. Restored and enlarged 1894–5 by S. Gambier-Parry.

CUTSDEAN, St. James. C14 tower, otherwise rebuilt in 1863.

DAGLINGWORTH, Holy Rood. Anglo Saxon sculptures and architecture; Norman and medieval. Restored 1845–50.

DAYLESFORD, St. Peter. 1860 by J.L. Pearson.

DEERHURST, St. Mary. Important Anglo-Saxon church. EE arcades. Stained glass.

DIDBROOK, St. George. c 1475. Perp tower.

DIDMARTON, St. Michael. 1872 by T.H. Wyatt.

DOWDESWELL, St. Michael. Norman and medieval. Cruciform plan. Monuments.

DOWN AMPNEY, All Saints. EE with C14 spire. Monuments. C19 furnishings.

DOWN HATHERLEY, St. Mary. Perp tower otherwise rebuilt in 1860 by Fulljames & Waller.

DRIFFIELD, St. Mary. Rebuilt in 1734 and again in 1863. C19 stained glass.

DRYBROOK, Holy Trinity. 1817.

DUMBLETON, St. Peter. Norman and medieval. Monuments.

DUNTISBOURNE ABBOTS, St. Peter. Anglo Saxon origin, and Norman. Restored 1872.

DUNTISBOURNE ROUSE, St. Michael. Anglo Saxon origin, and Norman. Wall painting.

DURSLEY, St. James. C13 and later. Tower early C18. Restored 1867 by Sir T.G. Jackson.
St. Mark, Woodmancote. 1844 by G. Alexander.

DYMOCK, St. Mary. Outstanding early Norman work. Restored c. 1870 by John Middleton; scraped.

EASTCOMBE, St. Augustine. 1868 by Rev. W.H. Lowder.

EASTINGTON, St. Michael. Medieval. C20 stained glass.

EASTLEACH, St. Andrew. Norman and EE.
St. Michael & St. Martin. Splendid Dec work. Setting. Threatened with redundancy.

EBRINGTON, St. Eadburga. Norman and medieval. Monuments.

EDGE, St. John the Baptist. 1865 by S.W. Daukes.

EDGEWORTH, St. Mary. Anglo-Saxon, Norman and medieval. Over-restored in C19.

ELKSTONE, St. John. Outstanding Norman work. Perp tower.

ELMORE, St. John the Baptist. EE. Monuments and table tombs.

ELMSTONE HARDWICKE, St. Mary Magdalene. Medieval. Perp tower.

ENGLISH BICKNOR, St. Mary. Norman and EE. Perp tower.

EVENLODE, St. Edward. Norman and medieval. C15 pulpit.

FAIRFORD, St. Mary. Superb medieval glass. Perp 'wool' church. Screen. Monuments and brasses.

FARMCOTE, St. Faith. Norman and Tudor. Furnishings and monument.

FARMINGTON, St. Peter. Norman. Perp tower.

FLAXLEY, St. Mary. 1856 by Sir Gilbert Scott.

FORTHAMPTON, St. Mary. Medieval. Restored and enlarged in C19. Good C19 stained glass.

FRAMILODE, St. Peter. 1854 by Francis Niblett.

FRAMPTON MANSELL, St. Luke. 1844 by J. Parish.

FRAMPTON-ON-SEVERN, St. Mary. Medieval. Restored in C19 with sanctuary by Henry Woodyer. Monuments.

FRANCE LYNCH, St. John the Baptist. 1855–7 by G.F. Bodley.

FRETHERNE, St. Mary. 1847 by Francis Niblett.

FROCESTER, St. Andrew. C17; restored in 1849.

GLOUCESTER, All Saints. 1875 by Sir Gilbert Scott.
Christ Church. 1822 by Rickman & Hutchinson.
St. Barnabas. 1939 by N.F. Cachemaille Day.
St. Catherine. 1915 by W.B. Wood.
St. James. 1841 by S. Kempthorne.
St. John the Baptist. 1734 by E. & T. Woodward.
St. Margaret. C13–14.
St. Mark. 1847 by Francis Niblett.
St. Mary de Crypt. Originally Norman. Important medieval and Perp work. Restored in 1844 by Daukes & Hamilton.
St. Mary de Lode. Norman, with nave added in 1826.
St. Mary Magdalene. Norman chancel only.
St. Michael. C15 tower only.
St. Oswald. 1939 by Ellery Anderson.
St. Paul. 1823 by C.N. Tripp.
St. Stephen. 1895 by W. Planck.

GORSLEY, Christ Church. 1892 by C., Rollinson.

GREAT WASHBOURNE, St. Mary. Norman; Chancel 1642.,

GREAT WITCOMBE, St. Mary. Norman and medieval. C18 tower.

GRETTON, Christ Church. 1868 by J.D. Wyatt.

GUITING POWER, St. Michael. Norman. Perp tower. Chancel rebuilt in 1903.

HAILES CHURCH. c. 1130. Unusual survivals including C15 screen, furnishings, wall-paintings, tiles and stained glass.

HAMPNETT, St. George. Norman, with vault. Perp tower. C19 wall painting.

HARDWICKE, St. Nicholas. Medieval but altered in C19. Monuments.

HARESCOMBE, St. John the Baptist. Medieval. C13 bellcote. Restored in 1871 by Francis Niblett.

HARESFIELD, St. Peter. Norman and medieval.

HARNHILL, St. Michael. Norman and medieval. Restored in 1909 by F.W. Waller.

HARTPURY, St. Mary. Norman. Perp tower. Restored in 1882.

HASELTON, St. Andrew. Norman with later alterations. Perp tower.

HASFIELD, St. Peter. Medieval. Restored c.1850 by T. Fulljames.

HATHEROP, St. Nicholas. Rebuilt 1854–5 by Henry Clutton and William Burges.

HAWLING, St. Edward. Rebuilt c. 1764. Georgian features survive. Norman remains. Perp tower.

HEMPSTED, St. Swithun. c. 1477. Restored C19.

HEWELSFIELD, St. Mary Magdalene. Norman and medieval. Restored 1863–7 by Butterfield.

HIGHNAM, Holy Innocents. 1849–51 by Henry Woodyer. Wall-paintings by Thomas Gambier-Parry.

HORSLEY, St. Martin. Perp tower, otherwise 1838–9 by Thomas Rickman.

HUCCLECOTE, St. Philip & St. James. 1850 by John Jacques.

HUNTLEY, St. John the Baptist. 1863 by S.S. Teulon.

ICOMB, St. Mary. EE. Restored 1871 by W.J. Hopkins.

KEMBLE, All Saints. C13 tower, otherwise rebuilt in 1872–8 by Medland & Son.

KEMPLEY, St. Edward the Confessor. 1903 by Randall Wells. 'Arts and Crafts' furnishings.

KEMPSFORD, St. Mary. Norman and medieval. Perp central tower. Restored by G.E. Street. Stained glass.

KINGSCOTE, St. John, Perp tower, otherwise mostly rebuilt by S.S. Teulon in 1851. Kingscote monuments.

KINGS STANLEY, St. George. Norman and medieval. Restored by G.F. Bodley in 1876.

KINGSWOOD, St. Mary. 1723, restored in 1900.

LASBOROUGH, St. Mary. 1861–2 by L. Vulliamy.

LECHLADE, St. Lawrence. Perp. Tower and spire.

LECKHAMPTON, St. Peter. Medieval. C14 central tower and spire. Rebuilt and enlarged 1866–8 by J. Middleton.
St. Philip & St. James. 1870 by J. Middleton.

LEIGH, St. Catherine. C13. Perp tower.

LEIGHTERTON, St. Andrew. Medieval. Restored in 1877 by Waller & Son.

LEONARD STANLEY, St. Swithin. Norman. Important remains of Priory. Chancel restored 1880 by G.F. Bodley.

LITTLE DEAN, St. Ethelbert. Norman and medieval.

LONGBOROUGH, St. James. Norman and medieval. Perp tower. Monuments.

LONGHOPE, All Saints. C13 but restored in 1869 by A.W. Maberley.

LONGLEVENS, Holy Trinity. 1935 by H. Stratton Davis.

LONGNEY, St. Laurence. Medieval. Restored 1873 by F.S. Waller.

LOWER LEMINGTON, St. Leonard. Norman and medieval.

LOWER SLAUGHTER, St. Mary. Rebuilt 1867 by B. Ferrey.

LYDBROOK, Holy Jesus. 1851 by Henry Woodyer.

LYDNEY, St. Mary. Medieval. Tower and spire.

MAISEMORE, St. Giles. Mostly rebuilt 1869 by Fulljames and Waller. Perp tower.

MATSON, St. Katherine. 1852 and 1893 by Waller & Son.

MEYSEY HAMPTON, St. Mary. Medieval, cruciform, good Dec. work. Monuments.

MICKLETON, St. Lawrence. Norman and medieval.

MINCHINHAMPTON, Holy Trinity. C12. Cruciform. Central tower. C14 transept. Monuments.

MINSTERWORTH, St. Peter. 1870 by Henry Woodyer.

MISERDEN, St. Andrew. Saxon and medieval. Restored in 1866 by Rev. W.H. Lowder. Monuments.

MITCHELDEAN, St. Michael. Medieval. Tower and spire.

MORETON-IN-MARSH, St. David. 1858 by Poulton & Woodman.

MORETON VALENCE, St. Stephen. Norman and medieval.

NAILSWORTH, St. George. 1898–1900 by M.H. Medland.

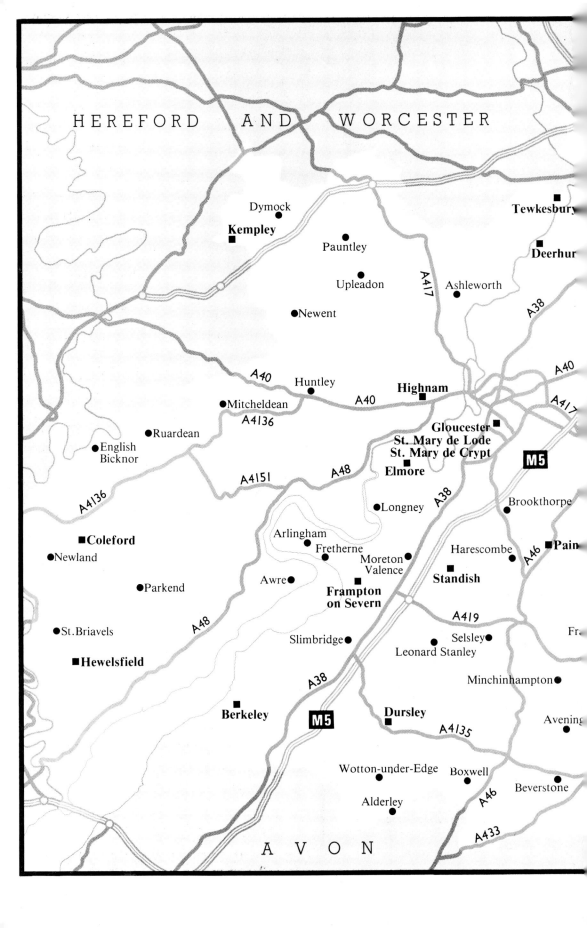

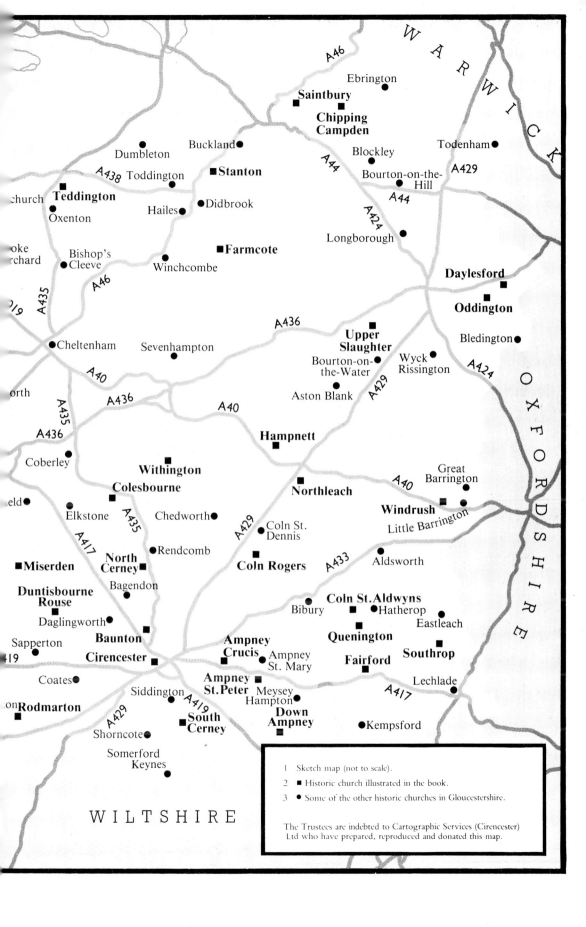

W A R W I C K

A46

Ebrington

Saintbury

Chipping Campden

Blockley

Todenham

A429

Buckland

Dumbleton

A438 Toddington

Stanton

Bourton-on-the-Hill

A44

A44

Teddington

church

Oxenton

Hailes

Didbrook

A424

Longborough

Daylesford

oke rchard

Bishop's Cleeve

Farmcote

Oddington

A435

A46

Winchcombe

Bledington

)19

A436

Upper Slaughter

Cheltenham

Sevenhampton

Bourton-on-the-Water

Wyck Rissington

A424

A40

A436

Aston Blank

A429

orth

A435

A436

A40

Hampnett

Great Barrington

A40

A436

Coberley

Withington

Northleach

Windrush

Little Barrington

eld

Colesbourne

Elkstone

A435

Chedworth

A429

Coln St. Dennis

Aldsworth

A417

Rendcomb

A433

■**Miserden**

North Cerney

Coln Rogers

Duntisbourne Rouse

Bagendon

Coln St.Aldwyns

Daglingworth

Bibury

Hatherop

Eastleach

Sapperton

Baunton

Quenington

Southrop

)19

Cirencester

Ampney Crucis

Ampney St. Mary

Fairford

Coates

Siddington

A419

Ampney St.Peter

Meysey Hampton

Lechlade

on**Rodmarton**

A429

South Cerney

Down Ampney

A417

Shorncote

Kempsford

Somerford Keynes

1   Sketch map (not to scale).

2   ■ Historic church illustrated in the book.

3   ● Some of the other historic churches in Gloucestershire.

The Trustees are indebted to Cartographic Services (Cirencester) Ltd who have prepared, reproduced and donated this map.

W I L T S H I R E

O X F O R D S H I R E

NAUNTON, St. Andrew. Medieval, Perp tower; restored C16.

NEWENT, St. Mary. Nave rebuilt in C17. Restored 1881 by J. Middleton. C14 tower and spire.

NEWLAND, All Saints. 'The Cathedral of the Forest'. Medieval. C14 tower. Restored 1861 by W. White. Monuments.

NEWNHAM-ON-SEVERN, St. Peter. 1847 by Waller.

NORTH CERNEY, All Saints. Norman and medieval. Furnishings including rood screen by F.C. Eden. Stained glass.

NORTHLEACH, St. Peter & St. Paul. Great 'wool' church of the C15. To be compared with Chipping Campden. Monuments and brasses.

NORTH NIBLEY, St. Martin. Medieval. Chancel rebuilt by J.L. Pearson in 1861.

NORTON, St. Mary. Medieval. Perp tower. Restored by Waller & Christian in 1875–6.

NOTGROVE, St. Bartholomew. Norman, probably Anglo-Saxon origin, and medieval. Restored by J.E.K. Cutts in 1873. Monuments.

NYMPSFIELD, St. Bartholomew. Perp tower, otherwise rebuilt in 1861–3 by S.S. Teulon.

OAKRIDGE, St. Bartholomew. 1837 by R. Stokes.

ODDINGTON, Holy Ascension. 1852 by S.W. Daukes, additions 1854–6, by J.L. Pearson. St. Nicholas. Norman and medieval. Furnishings. Wall paintings.

OLDBURY-ON-THE-HILL, St. Arild. Medieval. Perp tower.

OWLPEN, Holy Cross. Rebuilt 1828–30, and altered 1874–5 by J.P. St. Aubyn. Mosaics by Powell.

OXENHALL, St. Anne. Rebuilt 1865, by John Middleton, except for early C14 tower.

OXENTON, St. John the Baptist. Medieval, tactfully restored in 1905. Wall paintings. Perp tower.

OZLEWORTH, St. Nicholas. Norman. Hexagonal tower. Restored in C19 by Rev. W.H. Lowder. Redundant.

PAINSWICK, St. Mary. Medieval. Restored 1883 by Waller. Tower and spire. Churchyard.

PARKEND, St. Paul. 1822 by Rev. H. Poole. Classical.

PAUNTLEY, St. John. Norman and medieval. Perp tower.

PAXFORD, dedication unknown. 1866.

PITCHCOMBE, St. John the Baptist. 1819 and 1870.

POOLE KEYNES, St. Michael. c. 1770.

POULTON, St. Michael. 1873 by W. Butterfield.

PRESTBURY, St. Mary. Medieval. Restored in 1864 by G.E. Street.

PRESTON, All Saints. Medieval. C14 bellcote. Perp tower.

PRESTON, St. John the Baptist. Norman. South aisle added in 1859.

PRIMROSE HILL, Holy Trinity. 1903.

QUEDGELEY, St. James. C14 tower and spire. Largely rebuilt in 1856 by H. Woodyer

QUENINGTON, St. Swithin. Norman. Famous doorways and tympana.

RANDWICK, St. John. Perp tower. Restored 1865.

REDBROOK, St. Saviour. 1873 by J.P. Seddon.

REDMARLEY D'ABITOT, St. Bartholomew. 1738. Restored 1864–5 by Francis Niblett.

RENDCOMB, St. Peter. Early C16 Perp. Furnishings, screen, stained glass.

The **RISSINGTONS. GREAT RISSINGTON,** St. John the Baptist. Norman and medieval. Largely rebuilt in 1873.

LITTLE RISSINGTON, St. Peter. Norman. Restored in 1850 by Francis Niblett.

RODBOROUGH, St. Mary Magdalene. Rebuilt in 1842 except the Perp tower.

RODMARTON, St. Peter. Medieval. Tower and spire. Monuments.

RUARDEAN, St. John the Baptist. Norman and medieval. Restored in 1890 by Waller & Son. Tower and spire.

RUDFORD, St. Mary. Norman.

ST. BRIAVELS, St. Mary. Norman. Restored 1861.

SAINTBURY, St. Nicholas. Norman, cruciform and medieval. Arts and Crafts furnishings.

SALPERTON, All Saints. Norman and medieval. Wall painting. Restored 1855.

SANDHURST, St. Lawrence. Medieval tower, otherwise rebuilt in 1858.

SAPPERTON, St. Kenelm. C14 with Queen Anne alterations. Monuments and furnishings.

SAUL, St. James. Perp, altered and enlarged 1863–5 by T. Fulljames.

SELSLEY, All Saints. 1862 by G.F. Bodley. Stained glass by William Morris and Philip Webb.

SEVENHAMPTON, St. Andrew. Norman and EE, enriched and altered in C15. Churchyard.

SHEEPSCOMBE, St. John. c. 1820 and 1872 by F. Niblett.

SHERBORNE, St. Mary Magdalene. C14 tower and spire. Rebuilt c 1859. Monuments.

SHIPTON MOYNE, St. John the Baptist. Medieval, largely rebuilt 1864–5 by T.H. Wyatt.

SHIPTON OLIFFE, St. Oswald. Medieval. C13 bellcote. Restored 1903–4 by H.A. Prothero.

SHIPTON SOLLARS, St. Mary. C13. Restored in 1929.

SHORNCOTE, All Saints. Norman and medieval. C14 bellcote. Restored in 1882–3 by William Butterfield.

SHURDINGTON, St. Paul. Early C14 tower and spire. Medieval. C19 chancel.

SIDDINGTON, St. Peter. Norman. Beakheads and tympanum. Perp North aisle. Restored 1864 by Woodyer.

SLAD, Holy Trinity. 1831–4, restored by Benjamin Bucknall c. 1869.

SLIMBRIDGE, St. John. C13. Tower and spire. Carvings.

SNOWSHILL, St. Barnabus. 1864.

SOMERFORD KEYNES, All Saints. Saxon, and medieval. C18 tower. Restored 1875 by Waller.

SOUNDWELL, St. Stephen. 1903.

SOUTHAM, Ascension. Norman. Restored 1862.

SOUTH CERNEY, All Hallows. Norman, Transitional and Dec. Beakheads and tympanum comparable to Quenington. Central tower. Fragments of C12 Rood. Restored by St. Aubyn in 1862.

SOUTHROP, St. Peter. Norman, and medieval. Famous font.

STANDISH, St. Nicholas. Early C14. Tower and spire. Furnishings. Tombstones.

STANLEY PONTLARGE, dedication unknown. Norman. Much restored.

STANTON, St. Michael. Norman to Perp. Furnishings. Stained glass.

STANWAY, St. Peter. C12 but over-restored in 1896 by the incumbent, with 'friendly advice' from Sir A.W. Blomfield.

STAUNTON, All Saints. One of the ring of old churches round the Forest. Norman and medieval. Central tower.

STAUNTON, St. James. Norman, and medieval. Over-restored in 1860. C14 tower; but part of spire removed.

STAVERTON, St. Catherine. Medieval. Restored 1897.

STINCHCOMBE, St. Cyr. Mostly rebuilt in 1855 by J.L. Pearson.

STOKE ORCHARD, St. James the Great. Norman. Wall paintings.

STONE, All Saints. Medieval.

STONEHOUSE, St. Cyr. Perp tower, otherwise rebuilt in 1854.

STOWELL, St. Leonard. Norman. Cruciform. Wall paintings.

STOW-ON-THE-WOLD, St. Edward. Medieval and C17.

STRATTON, St. Peter. Norman. Much rebuilt 1850.

STROUD, St. Lawrence. Rebuilt 1866–8. C19 stained glass. Monuments.
        All Saints, Uplands. 1908–10 by Temple Moore.
        Holy Trinity. 1838 by Thomas Foster
        St. Alban 1915–16.

SUDELEY, St. Mary. Perp. c. 1460. Restored 1859–63 by Sir Gilbert Scott.

The **SWELLS. LOWER SWELL,** St. Mary. Norman. Enlarged 1852.

UPPER SWELL, St. Mary. Norman, and medieval.

SWINDON, St. Lawrence. Hexagonal Norman tower (c.f. Ozleworth). Otherwise rebuilt 1845 by T. Fulljames.

SYDE, St. Mary. Norman. C13/14 tower.

TARLTON, dedication unknown. Originally Norman, rebuilt 1875.

TAYNTON, St. Lawrence. Rebuilt by order of Parliament 1647–8. Restored by Fulljames, 1864.

TEDDINGTON, St. Nicholas. Norman. EE work from Hailes Abbey. Royal Arms.

TEMPLE GUITING, St. Mary. Norman, and medieval. Restored in C18 and in 1884.

TETBURY, St. Mary. 1781 by F. Hiorn. Tower and spire rebuilt in 1890.

TEWKESBURY, Abbey Church of St. Mary. Larger than many cathedrals but the parish church of Tewkesbury. Norman. The large Norman tower is an unusual survival. Choir and ambulatory of the apse remodelled in C14. Monuments. Stained glass.
Holy Trinity. 1837.

TIBBERTON, Holy Trinity. Norman and medieval.

TIDENHAM, St. Mary. EE and Dec. Over-restored 1858.
        St. Michael, Tidenham Chase. 1888 by S. Gambier-Parry.

TIRLEY, St. Michael. Medieval. Restored 1894.

TODDINGTON, St. Andrew. Rebuilt 1873–9 by G.E. Street.

TODENHAM, St. Thomas of Canterbury. C14. Splendid tower and spire.

TREDINGTON, St. John the Baptist. Norman and C16 furnishings. Stained glass.

TRESHAM, dedication unknown. 1855 Neo-Romanesque by J.J. Rowland.

TURKDEAN, All Saints. Norman and medieval.

TUTSHILL, St. Luke. 1853 by H. Woodyer.

TWIGWORTH, St. Matthew. 1842–4 by T. Fulljames.

TWYNING, St. Mary Magdalene. Norman. Restored in 1867–8 by John Middleton.

ULEY, St. Giles. 1857–8 by S.S. Teulon.

UP HATHERLEY, St. Philip & St. James. 1885 by Prothero & Phillott.

UPLEADON, St. Mary. Norman. Timber-framed tower of c. 1500. Restored 1879 by E. Christian.

UPPER SLAUGHTER, St. Peter. Norman. Altered in 1822 and restored 1877.

UPTON ST. LEONARDS. St. Leonard. Perp tower, otherwise mostly rebuilt in C19. Churchyard.

VINEY HILL, All Saints. 1867 by E. Christian.

WESTBURY-ON-SEVERN, Sts. Peter, Paul & Mary. Detached tower c. 1270, with C14 spire. Church medieval.

WESTCOTE, St. Mary. Mostly rebuilt in C19.

WESTONBIRT, St. Katherine. Medieval. Restored in C19.

WESTON-SUB-EDGE, St. John the Baptist. Perp tower; the rest restored 1861.

WHADDON, St. Margaret. Medieval. Restored 1855 and 1880.

WHELFORD, St. Anne. 1864 by G.E. Street.

WHITESHILL, St. Paul. 1839–41 by T. Foster.

WHITMINSTER, St. Andrew. Perp tower. Medieval. Restored in C19 by Sir A.W. Blomfield.

WHITTINGTON, St. Bartholomew. Norman and medieval. Restored 1872 by Waller. Monuments.

WILLERSEY, St. Peter. Norman and medieval.

WINCHCOMBE, St. Peter. c. 1465. Perp. Furnishings.

WINDRUSH, St. Peter. Norman. Famous doorway with beakheads. Restored by Woodyer.

WINSON, St. Michael. Norman. Churchyard.

WINSTONE, St. Bartholomew. Saxon and Norman.

WITHINGTON, St. Michael. Norman and Perp. Restored in 1872.

WOODCHESTER, St. Mary. 1863–4 by S.S. Teulon.

WOOLASTON, St. Andrew. Norman and medieval. Almost completely rebuilt 1859.

WOOLSTONE, St. Martin. medieval. Perp tower.

WORMINGTON, St. Catherine. c. 1475. Glass by William Morris. Monuments.

WOTTON-UNDER-EDGE, St. Mary. Medieval. Restored C18 and C19. Monuments. Perp tower.

WYCK RISSINGTON, St. Laurence. Norman and Transitional. Restored 1879.

YANWORTH, St. Michael. Norman. Restored in 1899 by Hodgson Fowler.

Roman Catholic Churches

CHELTENHAM, St. Gregory. 1854–7 by Charles Hansom.

CHIPPING CAMPDEN, St. Catherine. 1891 by W. Lunn.

CIRENCESTER, St. Peter. 1896 by A.J.C. Scoles.

FAIRFORD, Presbytery, Horcott. 1845.

GLOUCESTER, St. Peter. 1860–68 by G.R. Blount.

NYMPSFIELD, St. Joseph. C19/20

PAINSWICK, Friday Street. c. 1950 by Peter Falconer.

POSTLIP, St. James. Norman, restored 1890 by H.A. Prothero.

PRINKNASH, Chapel at Prinknash Park. Early C16. Stained glass.

STOW-ON-THE—WOLD, Our Lady and St Kenelm. 1918.

WINCHCOMBE, St Nicholas. 1915.

STROUD, Our Lady of the Immaculate Conception. 1858 by C.A. Buckler.

TETBURY, St. Michael's. C19.

WOODCHESTER. Priory Church of our Lady of the Annunciation. 1846–49, by Charles Hansom.

Nonconformist Places of Worship

Baptist Chapels

ARLINGTON. 1833.

AVENING. 1804, enlarged 1820.

BLOCKLEY. 1835.

BOURTON-ON-THE-WATER. 1877.

CHALFORD. 1870, enlarged 1810, became schoolroom 1895; new 1874.

CHELTENHAM. BETHEL, 1820 sold to Christadelphians.
     CAMBRAY. 1856 by Dangerfield.
     GAS GREEN.
     NORTH PLACE. Built for Countess of Huntingdon 1816, now independent Baptist.
     SALEM. 1844

CHIPPING CAMPDEN. 1872.

CINDERFORD. 1843.
    GREEN BOTTOM.
    STEAM MILLS.

CIRENCESTER. 1857.

COLEFORD. c. 1858, altered 1971.

EASTCOMBE. 1801, enlarged 1816, altered C20.

FRAMPTON MANSELL. 1960.

GUITING POWER. 1835.

KINGS STANLEY. 1825.

LECHLADE. 1825.

LECKHAMPTON. 1883.

LEIGHTERTON. 1828.

LONGHOPE. 1846.

LYDBROOK. c. 1830–35 (or rebuilt 1854?).

LYDNEY. c. 1834–7.

MINCHINHAMPTON. 1834, altered 1977.

NAILSWORTH. Re-erected on present site in 1881.

NAUNTON. 1831.

PAINSWICK. Built by Methodists 1806, taken over by Baptists in 1831.

PARKEND. 1862.

STOW-ON-THE-WOLD. 1852.

STROUD. 1824.

TETBURY. 1721.

TEWKESBURY. 1805.

WINSTONE. 1821–2.

WOODCHESTER. 1833.

WOTTON-UNDER-EDGE. 1818.

Redundant

TEWKESBURY. OLD MEETING. c. 1695.

United Reformed Church

BLAKENEY. c. 1923.

BRIERLEY. 1884.

CAM. Independent, c. 1702. Last restored 1933.

CHELTENHAM. St. Andrews, 1886.

Prestbury, 1866.

COLEFORD. Independent, 1804, rebuilt 1842.

DRYBROOK. 1858.

DURSLEY. QUARRY STREET. 1852.
          TABERNACLE. 1808; porch c. 1880.

FAIRFORD. 1853.

FRANCE LYNCH. 1819.

GLOUCESTER. BARTON STREET. 1893.
          James Forbes. 1872.

                    SOUTHGATE. Independent Evangelical.
                    ST. MARY'S. Countess of Huntingdon.

KINGSWOOD. 1821.

LITTLE DEAN. 1820.

MITCHELDEAN. c. 1822. Sold to Christian Fellowship.

MORETON-IN-MARSH. 1801, rebuilt c. 1896.

NEWENT. 1845.

NEWNHAM-ON-SEVERN. 1824?

PAINSWICK. 1803; porch and facade 1892; windows 1897–8 by William Morris & Co.

RODBOROUGH. 1837.

RUSCOMBE. 1828.

SHARPNESS. 1880.

STROUD. Bedford Street. 1837.

TETBURY. c. 1820 and 1862.

WORRALL HILL

WOTTON-UNDER-EDGE. OLD TOWN. 1701–3 altered in 1903.
                        TABERNACLE. Built by Rowland Hill c. 1773, rebuilt
                        1898. Redundant.

Methodist

BIRDWOOD. Early C19 for Countess of Huntingdon.

CINDERFORD. Wesleyan.

DURSLEY. 1864.

LYDBROOK, 1829, rebuilt.

STOW-ON-THE-WOLD. 1814, and 1865.

STROUD. ACRE STREET. 1763, enlarged 1796 now used by Salvation Army
            CASTLE STREET. 1876, by James Tait.

WINCHCOMBE. Rebuilt 1886.

Quaker Meeting Houses

CHIPPING CAMPDEN. c. 1757.

CIRENCESTER. 1673, altered 1726. Enlarged 1810, restored 1865.

NAILSWORTH. 1689.

PAINSWICK. 1705–6.

Unitarian Chapel

CIRENCESTER. 1672, restored 1891.